Dog ² Aug 2020

D1732690

Saving Travis
A Rescue Story —

Donation made in your 3yr Honor!

Written by
Rhea Sampson

Illustrated by
E.L. Scott

Be kind To Animals

♡ Rhea, Shannon & Travis

ISBN 978-1-7325944-0-1

Shannon picked up her leash and looked at Rhea.
Her eyes were pleading in a way Rhea immediately
understood. "OK, Shannon," she said. "Let's go for
a walk. John, are you coming too?"

1

So Rhea and John and Shannon went out for a walk.
Suddenly, Shannon ran into the bushes.

What did she see?

2

Out jumped a scruffy little dog! He didn't have a collar. Was he lost?

John approached the little dog, very slowly, and the little dog jumped into his arms.

John carried the little dog back home. Shannon wagged her tail. She had found a new friend! John said, "Let's call him Travis."

5

Rhea and John prepared a bowl of food
and another of water for the little dog, but they
suddenly couldn't find him anywhere!

They searched everywhere. Finally, with
Shannon's help, they found Travis' hiding place.
He was so scared!

Travis wolfed down his food and drank some water. He cried and whimpered as he ate. Then he crawled up on the couch and fell asleep. Rhea watched him closely and suddenly exclaimed, "Oh, no! He has fleas!"

So Rhea and John gave Travis a bath.
Travis was so much happier!

Did Travis belong to someone? What to do? Then they remembered what to do. They posted flyers on trees and poles all over their neighborhood. They also called the animal shelters to ask if anyone had lost a dog who looked like Travis.

Rhea and John took Travis to a veterinarian. Travis did not look well. The vet said, "He'll get his vaccinations, and he needs to have some teeth pulled, and he needs medicine for his skin. He should also be neutered."

John and Rhea didn't know how much
all of this was going to cost.
So their mother called
Palo Alto Humane Society.

The kind man who answered the telephone explained, "Yes, we can help! We have a special program for people who need extra help for their animals. This will help you pay for some of his care." Rhea's mother said, "Thank you!"

So everyone went to the animal hospital
to get help for Travis.

Travis's fur began to grow back, and he soon had a healthy coat. He could eat without crying out in pain. He gained weight and became a happy, healthy dog.

Travis and Shannon are now the best of friends. They play together and care for each other. Travis was very happy! He had found his forever home!

THE END